UNDERSTANDING
RELIGIONS

Initiation Customs

Katherine Prior

Wayland

Understanding Religions

Birth Customs
Death Customs
Food and Fasting
Initiation Customs
Marriage Customs
Pilgrimages and Journeys

About this book

This book is about growing up and becoming an adult member of a religion. Initiation ceremonies from six of the world's major religions are discussed.

Some of the chapters compare the ways in which children in different religions celebrate their entry into adulthood. There is a chapter which examines why some religions only have initiation ceremonies for boys and not for girls, and another considers the symbols and signs that different religions use in their initiation ceremonies.

The quotations from children and young adults who have been through initiation ceremonies will help younger readers to think about their own experiences with religion and imagine what it would be like to be growing up in another religion. Teachers will find that elements of each chapter can be used as starting points for discussion and further study.

Editor: Joanna Housley
Designer: Malcolm Walker

This edition published in 1995 by
Wayland (Publishers) Limited

First published in 1992 by
Wayland (Publishers) Limited
61 Western Road, Hove
East Sussex, BN3 1JD, England

British Library Cataloguing in Publication Data
Prior, Katherine
  Initiation Customs. (Understanding Religions Series)
  I. Title II. Series
  291.3

HARDBACK ISBN 0-7502-0423-0

PAPERBACK ISBN 0-7502-1668-9

Typeset by Kudos Editorial and Design Services
Printed in Italy by G Canale C.S.p.A. Turin

Contents

Growing up   4
Ages for initiation around the world   6
Initiation ceremonies for boys and girls   13
Preparing for an initiation ceremony   15
Symbols in initiation ceremonies   24
Celebrating initiation   29
Glossary   30
Further information   31
Index   32

Words that appear in **bold** in the text are
explained in the glossary on page 30.

Growing up

If you have a baby brother or sister you will know that newborn babies are helpless. They cannot do anything for themselves. They have to be fed and dressed by someone older, and someone always has to watch to see that they do not hurt themselves. Babies cannot tell right from wrong, so no one blames them if they spill their food or break their toys.

As babies get bigger and grow up into children they learn to look after themselves. Perhaps when you were four or five years old you learnt how to dress yourself and do up buttons and tie shoelaces. At school you learn how to read and write, while all the time your parents and other adults are teaching you what is good behaviour and what is bad behaviour. Learning these things is a part of growing up and becoming responsible for yourself. When you are fully grown up you will be an adult and you will have to make important decisions about your future.

Initiation ceremonies

In many religions there is a special **ceremony** to celebrate the time when a child is ready to become an adult. This is

Below Parents like to make sure that their children are taught about their own religion, and brought up to respect its beliefs and traditions.

Above As you grow up, besides learning different subjects at school, you learn about how to behave and how to make decisions for yourself.

called an initiation ceremony. The word 'initiation' means a beginning or an entry into something new, so an initiation ceremony is like a doorway into growing up. It marks a child's entry into adulthood. Children who are getting ready for their initiation ceremony are called initiates.

An initiation ceremony is a way of showing all the adults in the religious community that the girl or boy is ready to become a responsible member of their religion. After their initiation ceremony the initiates must accept full responsibility for their own behaviour and not allow their parents to take the blame for anything that they do wrong.

5

Ages for initiation around the world

If your family follows a religion closely you may have an initiation ceremony when you are older. Perhaps you or a friend have had one already. Different religions often have different ideas about how old children ought to be before they begin taking responsibility for their actions.

Left A Jewish boy reads from the Torah, the Jewish holy book, at his Bar Mitzvah.

A Jewish boy has his Bar Mitzvah in a **synagogue** on the first Saturday after his thirteenth birthday. A Jewish girl may have a Bat Mitzvah after her twelfth birthday. Jews believe that when a boy turns thirteen and a girl turns twelve they are old enough to understand and obey the Ten Commandments. These are the most important rules of Judaism. The words 'Bar Mitzvah' mean 'a son of the Commandments'. 'Bat Mitzvah' means 'a daughter of the Commandments'.

Amongst Christians, Roman Catholic children usually have their first **Holy Communion** when they are seven years old. This is a special meal of holy bread and wine which makes them a part of God's family. At the Communion

Right This Roman Catholic boy in Colombia is taking his first Holy Communion. It is an important event for him.

everyone joins together to give thanks that Jesus Christ came to earth to teach them to believe in God. They thank God for forgiving them for the bad things that they do.

Roman Catholics believe that when children reach the age of seven they are old enough to know the difference between right and wrong. That is why they take their first Holy Communion when they are seven. Later, when they are about twelve years old, they will have their **Confirmation** ceremony and become full adult members of the Church.

Anglicans and other **Protestant** children are older than Catholics when they have their initiation ceremonies.

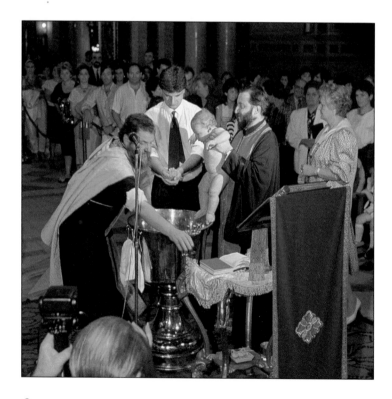

Left In the Greek Orthodox church babies are confirmed at the same time as they are **baptized**.

They have their Confirmation ceremony between the ages of twelve and sixteen, and often they only have their first Communion after they have been confirmed.

Orthodox Christian children are fully initiated into the Church while they are still babies. They have their Baptism and Confirmation ceremonies at the same time and often a parent or guardian takes their first Communion for them.

Muslims, like Roman Catholics, also believe that at the age of seven children are old enough to know the difference

Below This young Muslim boy in China is learning how to behave in a **mosque**.

between right and wrong. All Muslim parents know that their children's regular religious education should begin at the age of seven. When their children are about twelve or thirteen they are expected to know enough about their religion to behave like adult Muslims.

In Hinduism there is an initiation ceremony called the *Upanayana Samskara* or **Rite** of the Sacred Thread. Only boys who come from the top three **castes** in Hinduism have this ceremony. It is a very important occasion in their lives and is usually held when they are aged between eight and twelve. The exact

Left Many young Buddhist men and boys become monks. Here they are studying in a school in Thailand.

Udom is a Buddhist monk from Thailand. He had his *Pravrajya* ceremony when he was eighteen. He says:

'When I became a monk it was as if I had started my life all over again. Now, when people ask me how old I am, I say that I am thirteen because I have been living as a monk for thirteen years. At first it was very hard. I was used to going out and having lots of money. Now I can live in the **monastery** without any special things. If I have to go outside the monastery people look after me and help me with food and money for travelling.'

day for the ceremony must be a lucky one. It is chosen by an **astrologer**, who studies the movement of the planets and the stars. On the day that is chosen a Hindu boy has a thread tied on him that has been blessed by his priest. This is to show that he is starting a new, pure life. Hindus say that he has been reborn.

The only initiation ceremony in Buddhism is for people entering a monastery to begin training as a monk or a nun. Many more boys than girls do this and usually they are at least eight years old before they have the *Pravrajya* ceremony which marks the start of their new life as trainee monks.

Many *Pravrajya* ceremonies, especially in Burma and Thailand, are for boys who are only joining a monastery for a few months before they begin working and earning their own living. Their short time as a monk teaches them that it is possible to live a simple life without modern, expensive things like cars and radios.

Sikh children need to be at least fourteen years old before they can be baptized in an *Amrit* ceremony and welcomed as adult members of Sikhism. Sikhs think that children who are younger than fourteen are not able to understand the importance of a promise to obey the rules of their religion.

Manjeet, a Sikh girl, talks about the *Amrit* ceremony:

'My sister had her *Amrit* ceremony when she was sixteen. It was held in the spring, like a lot of them are in India. The first Sikhs were baptized in the spring so that's why we do it then – it's a way of remembering them. I'm thirteen, and I shan't be baptized for a few years. My parents say that I should wait until I'm ready to do it, and that I really know what I'm taking on.'

Initiation ceremonies for boys and girls

Above Many of the students at this Indian university are Hindu girls. Nowadays, instead of getting married when they are young, many go to universities or get jobs, and are responsible for their own futures.

Some religions have not always held initiation ceremonies for girls as well as boys. In the past, Hindu and Jewish girls never had initiation ceremonies. They got married when they were very young and their wedding was the only ceremony they had to show their community that they had grown up. Jewish and Hindu girls did not have responsibility for themselves, because they were always under the care of their parents or their husbands.

New ceremonies for girls

In some countries today Jewish and Hindu girls often do take responsibility for themselves. Not all of them get married while they are still teenagers. Many get jobs to support themselves or go on to university after they have finished school. Because of these changes many modern Jewish families like to have an initiation ceremony for girls too. This is called a Bat Mitzvah. In the synagogue, the girl says a special prayer on the Sabbath after her twelfth birthday.

In Buddhism only a few girls ever become nuns, so most of the girls do not have a proper initiation ceremony. In Burma, however, a Buddhist girl has her own special celebration of growing up. On the day of her brother's *Pravrajya* she is dressed up in expensive clothes and has her ears pierced with a golden needle. This Ear-Boring Ceremony is a way of telling everybody that one day she will get married and put on the fine jewellery that married Burmese women wear.

Left Buddhist nuns do not have the same initiation ceremonies as Buddhist monks do, but they are expected to lead the same, simple life.

Preparing for an initiation ceremony

Learning

Becoming a full member of a religious community often requires a lot of studying. Every religion has its own rules, prayers and **scriptures** which adult members should know and obey. An initiation ceremony is the time for boys

Right Jewish boys have to learn to read the Torah in the language of Hebrew. This means having special lessons before they have to read a passage from the Torah at their Bar Mitzvah.

David, a young Jewish man, remembers his Bar Mitzvah:

'I was really nervous when I had to do the reading. I knew how important it was because they don't let children read from the Torah. But even though I'd practised my piece over and over again, I was still afraid that I'd make a mistake in front of everyone. It was a big relief when it was over and we could have the party afterwards.'

and girls to show the adults in their community that they have started learning these things.

A Jewish boy studies hard for his Bar Mitzvah. At the ceremony he will be asked to read a section from the Torah, the Jewish scriptures which are written in the ancient language of Hebrew. Jews who live in Israel speak Hebrew, but for many Jewish children from other countries, learning to read the Torah is like learning a foreign language. Several times a week they attend special classes to study Hebrew and the history of Judaism.

Muslim children should be able to

read their holy book, the Qur'an, in its original language of Arabic. If they are growing up in countries where Arabic is not spoken, their parents, like Jewish parents, make special arrangements for them to learn to read the language.

When they are seven years old, Muslim children learn about religious beliefs, and are taught the correct way of praying and how to behave in a mosque. The history of Islam's holy days and **fasts** is explained to them and they begin to learn verses from the Qur'an by heart. They must know these things if they are to be respected as Muslims when they grow up.

Ishfaq, a Muslim boy from Pakistan, remembers his first lessons clearly:
'Not long after I was seven my parents hired a **mullah** to come to our house twice a week to teach my brother and me verses from the Qur'an. He was a very old man and he used to frown at me when I giggled. Nasir, my brother, was very good at his lessons, but the priest used to tell me that I was stupid. We didn't know any Arabic so it was very hard trying to remember the verses from one week to the next. My grandmother used to give me little tests in them and if I got one right she would feed me sweets and milk.'

For Sikhs too, it is important to be able to read the Sikh holy book, the Guru Granth Sahib, in its original language of Punjabi. If, at the time of their baptism into Sikhism, initiates do not know Punjabi they have to promise to learn it as soon as possible. Already they should have learnt the history of Sikhism's first leaders, the ten holy **Gurus**, and Sikhism's rules of dress and behaviour.

Christian children who are getting ready for their first Communion or Confirmation ceremony do not have to study Hebrew and Greek (the languages their holy book, the Bible, was written in) to be able to read the Bible. It is all

Above Sikhs are expected to be able to read their holy book, the Guru Granth Sahib, in Punjabi, the language in which it was written. In a gurdwara (Sikh temple) all events take place in front of the holy book.

right for them to read it in the language which is commonly used in their country. Usually, however, they attend special classes run by their priest or minister to help them understand the meanings of what is written in the Bible. They also learn about beliefs and ways of worship.

Right Christians can read their holy book, the Bible, in their own language. The Bible teaches them how to behave and worship as Christians.

In the past, a Hindu boy's *Upanayana Samskara* used to mark the beginning of his serious study of his religion. After he had put on the sacred thread he would go to live for some years with a guru, who would guide him in the study of Hinduism's ancient writings in **Sanskrit**. Nowadays it is more common for a Hindu boy just to learn a few prayers from his family's priest at the time of his initiation.

Before a Buddhist boy can be accepted into a monastery as a trainee or **novice** monk he has to learn the **Ten Precepts** (rules of behaviour) that guide the lives of all Buddhist monks. These rules tell him that he must not wear fancy clothes, sleep in a comfortable bed, go to films or dances, have a girlfriend or even handle any money while he is in the monastery. At the *Pravrajya* ceremony the senior monks will ask him whether he is prepared to join a monastery. In reply he will promise to obey the Ten Precepts and tell the senior monks that he is ready to lead the quiet and simple life of a monk.

Below   These novice monks in Burma are learning how to follow the Buddha's teaching while they are still very young. They are already wearing orange robes and are carrying bowls to collect food.

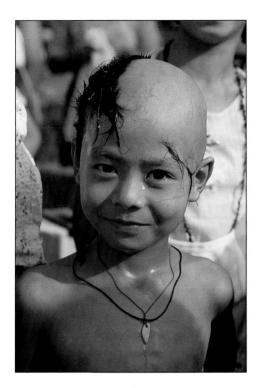

Above A Buddhist boy has his head shaved as part of his initiation into becoming a monk. Removing all the hair is a **symbol** for removing any sins of the past and starting a fresh life.

Dressing up

In many religions bathing and wearing special clothes are important parts of an initiation ceremony. They show everybody that the children who are being initiated have been preparing themselves properly for this occasion.

Hindu and Buddhist boys have special baths and have their heads shaved for their initiation ceremonies. Buddhist girls who are becoming nuns also have their heads shaved. They need to remove all dirt and impurities before they can start on their new, adult lives.

When a Buddhist boy or girl is about to enter a monastery he or she has to put on the plain **robe** that is worn by the monks or nuns there. In Thailand, Burma, Sri Lanka and India they wear deep yellow or orange-coloured robes. But Tibetan monks wear reddish-brown ones, Chinese and Korean monks wear grey ones, and Japanese monks wear black ones. In each of these countries the people are always able to recognize Buddhist monks and nuns because of these robes and their shaven heads.

Following rules of dress

Sikh initiates dress especially carefully for an *Amrit* ceremony. First they bathe and wash their hair. Then they put on their clothes, obeying the five rules of dress that mark Sikhs out from other

people. Their hair must be uncut, but worn neatly with a small comb tucked in it. They put on a pair of short pants under their clothes and a steel bangle around their arm, and tuck a small sword into some part of their dress. They must check that they are not wearing any jewellery or charms that belong to another religion. Once they have become adult Sikhs they must obey these rules for the rest of their lives.

At his Bar Mitzvah a Jewish boy wears a prayer shawl for the first time. It is called a *tallit*. Only adults wear these, so it is a sign that he has become an adult in the eyes of his community. From now on

Above At a Sikh *Amrit* ceremony five people represent the five 'beloved ones', who were the first members of the Sikh brotherhood.

Above After his Bar Mitzvah a Jewish boy can wear *tefillin* on his forehead and left arm.

he may also wear little black leather boxes on his left arm and on his forehead at the morning services in the synagogue. These are called *tefillin*. Inside them are pieces of paper which have sentences from the Torah written on them.

Roman Catholic girls often wear very special dresses for their first Communions. They are white, like a bride's dress, and sometimes they have little veils to cover the face and hair. White is a colour of purity and cleanliness. It is meant to show that the girls' hearts are clean as well as their bodies.

Right This group of Catholic girls in Poland are dressed for their first Communion. They wear white dresses as a symbol of purity.

Symbols in initiation ceremonies

What is a symbol?

Whenever we use actions or things instead of words to send a message we are using symbols. A traffic light is a symbol. When it turns to red we know to stop. When it changes to green we know that it is all right to go. Often symbols can be more useful than words, because they can be understood by people who come from different parts of the world and speak different languages.

Religions use many symbols. A religion may have followers living all over the world but all of them will recognize and understand their religion's symbols. Often symbols are very old; they carry messages across time as well as countries. The cross has been used as a symbol of Christianity for almost 2,000 years. The crescent (new) moon has been a symbol of Islam for over 1,300 years.

The symbols that are used in initiation ceremonies tell us a lot about a religion's beliefs and its history.

In a Christian Confirmation ceremony the bishop or minister who is leading

Above The Islamic symbol of a crescent moon is shown on these flags from the Maldive Islands.

the ceremony places his hands gently on the head of the initiates and welcomes them into God's family. This is called 'the laying on of hands' and it is a way of showing that the spirit of God has entered into the new adult members of the Church through the minister.

Extra symbols are used in Roman Catholic Confirmation ceremonies. Before the laying on of hands the bishop lightly slaps each initiate's face as a reminder to them that being a good Christian is difficult and sometimes involves hard decisions. The bishop then dips his right thumb in a sweet-smelling oil called chrism and makes the sign of

Anne-Marie, a Catholic girl, remembers:

'I was eleven when I was confirmed and I didn't know what to expect. We'd all discussed it at school and we were sure that the Bishop was really going to slap us hard. I was even afraid that the oil would be so hot that I would be stuck with the burn mark of a cross on my forehead for ever! Luckily it wasn't that bad. I even managed to get through the day without ripping my white dress.'

the cross on the forehead of the initiate, saying 'Be sealed with the gift of the Holy Spirit.' **Anointing** someone with oil is another way of showing that they have become a member of God's family.

Sikhs use a special liquid as a symbol in their initiation ceremonies too. It is called *amrit* or nectar. It is a sweet, slightly sticky mixture of water and sugar which the Sikhs have used in initiation ceremonies ever since Guru Gobind Singh welcomed the first five men into the Sikh brotherhood almost three hundred years ago. At an *Amrit* ceremony the *amrit* is prepared in a steel bowl by five Sikhs who symbolize these first five initiates. They stir it with short swords while prayers are being read from the Guru Granth Sahib. The people who are being initiated into Sikhism are given some *amrit* to drink and more is sprinkled on their eyes and hair. The *amrit* is a symbol of **immortality**, or everlasting life. It promises the initiates that if they obey the teaching of the Gurus their spirits will live for ever, even after their bodies have died.

Many of the symbols used in a Buddhist boy's *Pravrajya* ceremony contain messages about the new, simple life that he is beginning as a monk. In Burma, where initiation ceremonies are often grand and expensive occasions, the initiate acts out the life history of the

Above At a Sikh *Amrit* ceremony the initiate drinks a mixture of water and sugar from a steel bowl. The person being initiated does not have to be a child – this man is being initiated because he did not have an *Amrit* ceremony when he was younger.

Buddha. The Buddha was a prince who lived over two thousand years ago. He gave up his royal life in his father's palace to become a poor, holy man.

A Burmese boy who is being initiated is dressed up like a prince. He leads a big, noisy procession through his town's streets to the monastery where he asks the assembled monks to be allowed to

Right This Buddhist boy has been dressed in rich clothes, like a prince's. He will be led through the town on the donkey and will have to change into a monk's robe and have his head shaved before he is allowed to enter the monastery.

join them. First, however, he must take off his princely clothes and put on the plain, orange robe of a monk. Then his head and eyebrows are shaved. This is a symbol that he is leaving behind the ordinary world where people worry about their personal appearance. After he has **vowed** to obey the Ten Precepts and be a good monk he is given a new name from the ancient Buddhist language of Pali. This too is a symbol that he is starting a new life. He will use this name for as long as he is a monk. Sometimes his parents give him simple presents for his life in the monastery: another robe, sandals, and a bowl for collecting food.

There are two important symbols in a Hindu boy's initiation ceremony: the sacred fire and the sacred thread. The fire is a symbol of energy and purity and the priest prays in front of it before he takes up the sacred thread. This is a long white cotton cord tied into a loop with a special knot called the spiritual knot. The priest loops the cord over the boy's left shoulder and under his right arm. As long as the boy wears the cord it is a symbol that he has been born again as a high-caste Hindu. The priest then teaches him a short, special prayer called the *Gayatri Mantra*. Only boys and men who have had the *Upanayana* ceremony are allowed to hear this prayer.

Above This Hindu boy is wearing the sacred thread that has been tied around him at his *Upanayana Samskara*.

Celebrating initiation

The welcoming of a new adult member into a religious community is an occasion for everyone to celebrate. Family and friends come along to watch and often an important religious leader is invited to lead the ceremony. It is important that people attend an initiation ceremony because it shows the community that the child is now responsible. In many religions there is a big party after the ceremony, where everyone congratulates the boy or girl on growing up and praises the parents for having raised their child successfully.

Ravi, a Hindu boy, says:
'I was really surprised at all the people who turned up at my *Upanayana* ceremony. I had no idea that we had so many relations. My parents had set up a huge tent and hired caterers to cook for all the people. All my aunts made a big fuss of me. After they'd finished with me, I really did feel like a new person.'

Glossary

Amrit   A mixture of water and sugar used in Sikh initiation ceremonies.

Anointing   Putting holy oil on a person's head in a religious ceremony.

Astrologer   Someone who tells fortunes by studying the movement of planets.

Baptize   To sprinkle a person with, or immerse someone in, water, as a sign that he or she is cleansed from sin, and accepted as a member of the Christian Church.

Caste   A social group or class of Hindus.

Ceremony   A formal act, often carried out as part of a custom.

Confirmation   The Christian ceremony in which people become full members of the Church.

Fasts   Times when people go without food.

Gurus   Holy teachers in Hinduism or Sikhism.

Holy Communion   A service in which Christians take bread and wine to remember Christ's Last Supper.

Immortality   Everlasting life.

Monastery   A building where monks, and sometimes nuns, live, separate from the rest of a community.

Mosque   A Muslim place of worship.

Mullah   An Islamic teacher.

Novice   A beginner or trainee.

Protestant   A Christian who is not a member of the Roman Catholic or Orthodox Church.

Rite   A religious ceremony or ritual.

Robe   A long, single piece of cloth, wrapped around the body as clothing.

Sanskrit   The ancient language of Hinduism.

Scriptures   Holy books or sacred writings.

Symbol   Something that represents or stands for something else.

Synagogue   A place of worship for Jews.

Ten Precepts   The ten basic rules of behaviour observed by Buddhist monks.

Vowed   Made a solemn promise.

Further information

Books to read

Initiation Rites by Jon Mayled (Wayland, 1986)
Growing up in Hinduism by Jacqueline Hirst (with Geeta Pandey) (Longman, 1990)

The following series cover many aspects of different religions, including initiation customs:
Living the Faith (Oliver and Boyd, 1990)
Religions of the World (Simon and Schuster, 1992)

Picture acknowledgements

The publishers wish to thank the following for supplying the photographs in this book:
J Allan Cash 24; Cephas Picture Library 5 (Stuart Boreham), 13 (Pradip Mazumder); Eye Ubiquitous 14, 19 (C Skjold); Chris Fairclough Colour Library 22, 26; Sally and Richard Greenhill 17; Derek Henderson 18; Hutchison Library 7, 9 & 11 (both Liba Taylor), 20, 21, 27, 28 & 29 (both Liba Taylor); Life File 10 (Andrew Watson); Ann & Bury Peerless 6; Picturepoint cover; Reflections Photo Library 16 (John Downer); Topham 15, 25; Wayland Picture Library 12; Zefa 8, 23 (both).

Index

Numbers in **bold** indicate photographs

Amrit ceremony   12, 21-22, **22**, 26, 26

Arabic   17

Bar Mitzvah   **6**, 6-7, **16**, 16, 22
baptism   **8**, 9
Bat Mitzvah   6-7, 13, 16
Bible, the   18-19, **19**
Buddha, the   27
Burma   11, 14, 21, 26, 27

Communion   **7**, 7-8, 9, 18
Confirmation   8, 9, 18, 24, **25**, 25

ear-boring ceremony   14

Gayatri Mantra   28
Greek   18
Guru Granth Sahib   **18**, 18
Gurus
   Sikh   18, 26
   Hindu   19

head-shaving   **21**, 21, 28
Hebrew   16, 18

laying on of hands   25

monks, Buddhist   10, **11**, 11-12, **20**, 20, 26, 27
mullah   17

nuns, Buddhist   11, **14**, 21

Orthodox Christians   9

Pakistan   17
Pali   28
Pravrajya   11, 20, 26
Protestants   8-9
Punjabi   18

Qur'an   **17**, 17

Roman Catholics   7-8, 9, **23**, 23, **25**, 25

sacred thread   9, 10, 19, 28, **28**
Sanskrit   19

tallit   22
tefillin   **23**, 23
Ten Precepts   20, 28
Thailand   11, 21
Torah   **16**, 16, 23

Upanayana samskara   10, 19, 28, 29